Text copyright © Sept 2022 **Carmen Martínez Jover**
www.carmenmartinezjover.com

Illustrations copyright © 2022 **Rosemary Martínez**
www.rosemarymartinez.com

ISBN: 978-607-29-3616-4

Our ROPA Journey, a lesbian parenting story
Reception of Oocytes from Partner method

1st edition October 2023

Story: Carmen Martínez Jover
Design & illustrations: Rosemary Martínez
Layouts: Víctor Alfonso Nieto

More Books: www.fertilitybooks.net

Personalise books for your kids with your own family names for boys, girls and
twins: https://books.carmenmartinezjover.com

We dedicate this book to
all those amazing women
creating families.

Carmen & Rosemary
Martínez Jover

Our ROPA Journey

Written by
Carmen Martinez Jover

Illustrated by
Rosemary Martinez

Once upon a time there were two cats: Maty and Anya.

They lived very happily in their cozy home.

One day they were in
the park watching all
the tiny kittens playing
around them.

Maty said,
"Wouldn't it be lovely
to have our own
tiny kitten."

"Let's see," said Maty, "we both have a womb and tiny itsy bitsy eggs to conceive our own tiny kitten, what we are missing is a sperm."

"Let's both participate in giving birth to our tiny kitten!" said Anya full of enthusiasm.

"Maty, we can
use your egg...
an egg

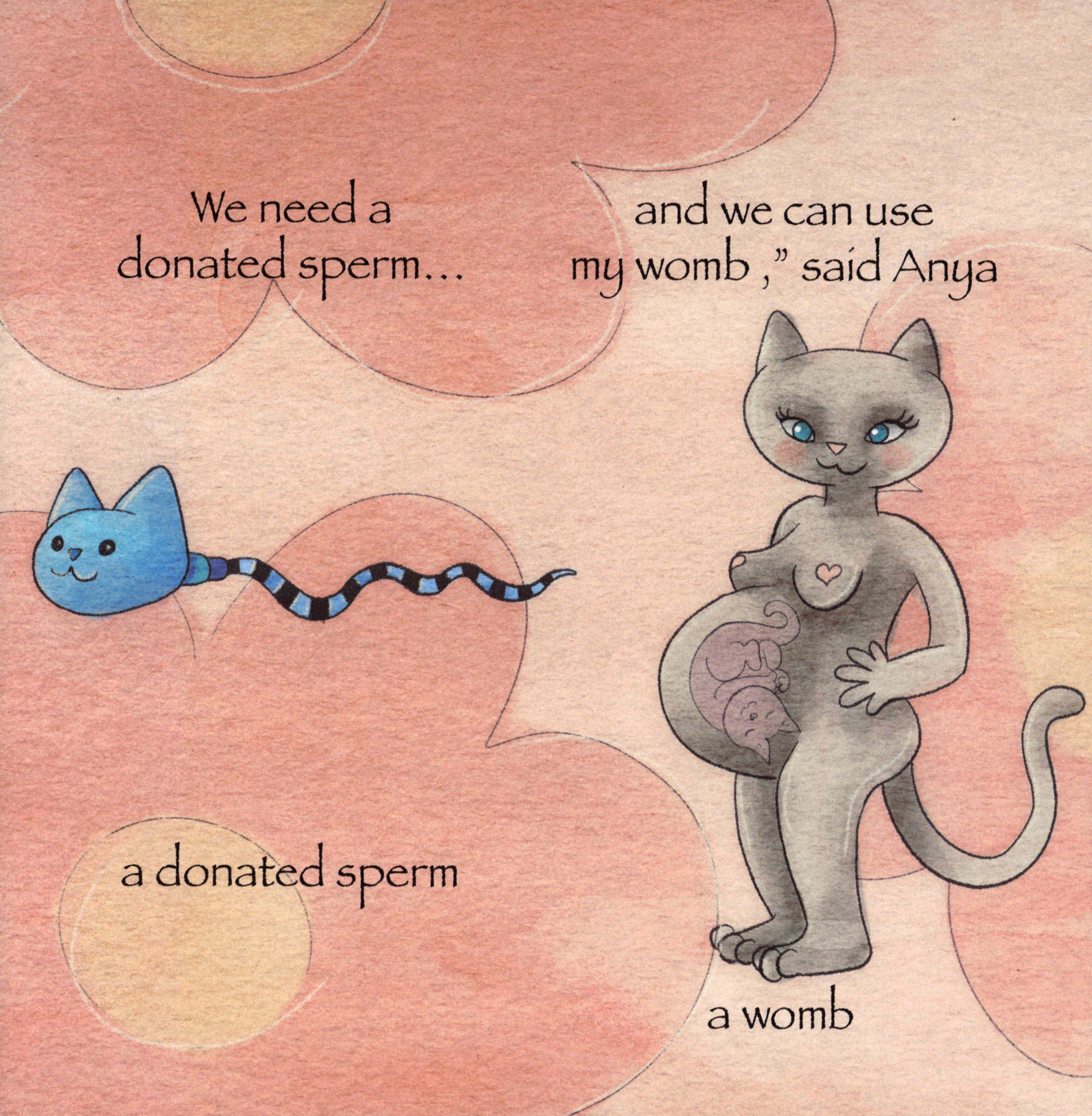

We need a
donated sperm...
and we can use
my womb ," said Anya
a donated sperm
a womb

"Let's make a list. We have your
tiny itsy bitsy egg and
we have my womb,"
said Anya as she wrote
on a piece of paper.

"Wonderful!" replied Maty,
"Let's go and find a
donated sperm."

Our ROPA Journey
Find an egg
"A seed which comes from a female cat".
Find a womb
"which is in a female cat".
Find sperm
"Seed which comes from a male cat".

Maty and Anya started
searching for their
sperm donor.

Catgle
98%
Clinic Vitro
Dr Qmthm Om

Their research took them
to a sperm bank where
they were given many
options of possible
sperm donors.

Anya and Maty both carefully chose who would be the best sperm donor for their tiny kitten.

In the clinic, the doctor gently put Maty's egg and the donated sperm together in a test tube and patiently looked after them until they fertilized and became one, forming an embryo, which is the beginning of a baby.

When the embryo started to grow, The doctor placed it carefully into Anya's womb.

The doctor explained that using one mother's egg and the other mother's womb is known as ROPA*.

*Reception of Oocytes from Partner method

Soon Anya's tummy started to grow
and grow
and grow.

Maty would always look after her.

Anya liked eating lots of
delicious things so that
their tiny kitten would
grow very
healthy.

Finally Maty and Anya had their
tiny kitten, and do you know what?
KIT
was the most beautiful adorable
kitten you had ever seen.

KIT grew…
and grew…
and grew…

and they lived happily
ever after as a family.

EGG DONATION

A tiny itsy bitsy gift of life, an egg donor story for girls, boys and twins.

EGG AND SPERM DONATION

Two tiny itsy bitsy Gifts of Life, an egg and sperm donor story.

SINGLE MUM BY CHOICE

Forever together, a single mum by choice story for one child or twins.

TWO MUMS   ADOPTION   TWO DADS

  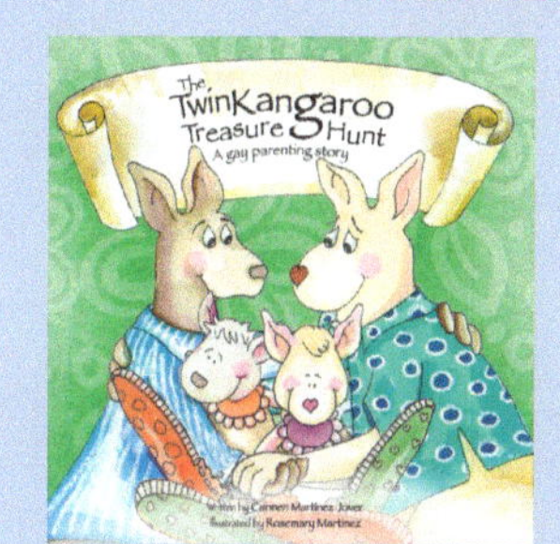 

Our ROPA Journey
a lesbian parenting story

Soul's time to be born,
an adoption story.

The baby kangaroo treasure hunt,
a gay parenting story for one child or twins.

Other books by: Rosemary & Carmen Martinez Jover

 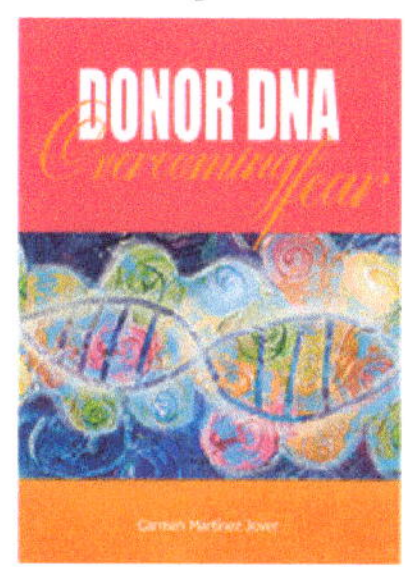  

**I want to have a child,
whatever it takes!**

**Donor DNA,
overcoming fear**

**Recipes of How Babies
are Made**

**Bloom, wherever you
may be planted**